Psalm 118 Fulfilled

Psalm 118 Fulfilled

Gaile Thulson

Cup of Water Publishing

PSALM 118 FULFILLED
Copyright © 2022 by Gaile Thulson

All Rights Reserved.
No part of this book may be reproduced, scanned, or distributed in any printed or electronic form without permission.

Scriptures taken from the Holy Bible, New International Version®, NIV®. Copyright © 1973, 1978, 1984, 2011 by Biblica, Inc.™ Used by permission of Zondervan. All rights reserved worldwide. www.zondervan.com The "NIV" and "New International Version" are trademarks registered in the United States Patent and Trademark Office by Biblica, Inc.™

Cover design © 2022 by Cup of Water Publishing, LLC

Cover image:
 La Cène (The Last Supper), 1896
 Pascal Dagnan-Bouveret (1852–1929)
 Public domain

ISBN 979-8-9863406-3-0 (Hardcover)
ISBN 979-8-9863406-4-7 (Paperback)
ISBN 979-8-9863406-5-4 (eBook)

To the author and
finisher of our faith

Psalm 118 Fulfilled

Psalm 118
(New International Version)

¹ *Give thanks to the L*ORD *[YHWH], for he is good;*
his love endures forever.

² *Let Israel say:*
"His love endures forever."
³ *Let the house of Aaron say:*
"His love endures forever."
⁴ *Let those who fear the L*ORD *say:*
"His love endures forever."

⁵ *When hard pressed, I cried to the L*ORD*;*
he brought me into a spacious place.
⁶ *The L*ORD *is with me; I will not be afraid.*
What can mere mortals do to me?
⁷ *The L*ORD *is with me; he is my helper.*
I look in triumph on my enemies.

⁸ *It is better to take refuge in the L*ORD
than to trust in humans.
⁹ *It is better to take refuge in the L*ORD
than to trust in princes.
¹⁰ *All the nations surrounded me,*
*but in the name of the L*ORD *I cut them down.*
¹¹ *They surrounded me on every side,*
*but in the name of the L*ORD *I cut them down.*
¹² *They swarmed around me like bees,*
but they were consumed as quickly as burning thorns;
*in the name of the L*ORD *I cut them down.*
¹³ *I was pushed back and about to fall,*
*but the L*ORD *helped me.*
¹⁴ *The L*ORD *is my strength and my defense*[a]*;*
he has become my salvation.

¹⁵ *Shouts of joy and victory*
resound in the tents of the righteous:
*"The L*ORD*'s right hand has done mighty things!*
¹⁶   *The L*ORD*'s right hand is lifted high;*
*the L*ORD*'s right hand has done mighty things!"*
¹⁷ *I will not die but live,*
*and will proclaim what the L*ORD *has done.*
¹⁸ *The L*ORD *has chastened me severely,*

but he has not given me over to death.
¹⁹ *Open for me the gates of the righteous;*
   I will enter and give thanks to the LORD.
²⁰ *This is the gate of the LORD*
   through which the righteous may enter.
²¹ *I will give you thanks, for you answered me;*
   you have become my salvation.

²² *The stone the builders rejected*
   has become the cornerstone;
²³ *the LORD has done this,*
   and it is marvelous in our eyes.
²⁴ *The LORD has done it this very day;*
   let us rejoice today and be glad.

²⁵ *LORD, save us!*
   LORD, grant us success!

²⁶ *Blessed is he who comes in the name of the LORD.*
   From the house of the LORD we bless you.[b]
²⁷ *The LORD is God,*
   and he has made his light shine on us.
  With boughs in hand, join in the festal procession
   up[c] *to the horns of the altar.*

²⁸ *You are my God, and I will praise you;*
you are my God, and I will exalt you.

²⁹ *Give thanks to the L*ORD*, for he is good;*
his love endures forever.

Footnotes

a. Psalm 118:14 Or *song*
b. Psalm 118:26 The Hebrew is plural.
c. Psalm 118:27 Or *Bind the festal sacrifice with ropes / and take it*

Introduction

When they had sung a hymn,
they went out to the Mount of Olives.
Matthew 26:30, Mark 14:26

Psalm 118 is sometimes mentioned as the last Passover hymn sung by our Lord before his betrayal. This is generally made as a passing comment that remains unexplained and undeveloped.

Why was it sung every Passover? *Why* was it the last hymn sung by our Lord? Did Psalm 118 have any special significance to Jesus on this night? Later, when they more fully understood, would it have had any special significance to the apostles as they reflected on the events that followed? Should it have any special significance to us, his followers, as we look back at the Passion, crucifixion, and resurrection?

I believe Psalm 118 to be central to our understanding of Easter. *This* is the hymn Jesus sang as he went out to fulfill the old covenant by giving his life.

This is the hymn Jesus sang after giving his disciples the new covenant based on his broken body and spilled blood. The Jewish day actually begins at sundown, so *this* is the hymn Jesus sang on the day he was crucified.

Imagine Jesus singing these words as he was about to go to his death. When this perspective is used as the lens through which we read and interpret Psalm 118 there is a richness to the psalm otherwise lost. It is not a coincidence that *this* psalm is the one he sang. God had it in his plan from the beginning and it was in place at the right time, when needed by his Son. *This* is the psalm Jesus fulfilled on the cross. He did it out of love for the Father and love for us.

The Call to Praise (v. 1)
All Who Know God's Lovingkindness (vv. 2–4)
The L̲o̲r̲d̲ is with Me in My Distress (vv. 5–7)
Put Your Trust in God, Not Humans (vv. 8–9)
Surrounded by Enemies, the L̲o̲r̲d̲ Helped Me
 (vv. 10–12)
The L̲o̲r̲d̲ has Become My Salvation (vv. 13–14)
The Strong Right Hand of the L̲o̲r̲d̲ (vv. 15–16)
I Will Not Die but Live (vv. 17–21)
The Rejected Stone Becomes the Cornerstone
 (vv. 22–24)

LORD Save Us! (vv. 25–26)
Taking the Sacrifice to the Altar (vv. 27–28)
The Final Call to Praise (v. 29)

The Call to Praise
(Psalm 118:1)

Give thanks to the Lord, for he is good;
his love endures forever.

This psalm is categorized as a psalm of praise, however it is a very special psalm of praise related to the crucifixion and resurrection of Jesus Christ. Every year at Passover, Jesus sang the songs of the Great Hallel (Great Praise) consisting of Psalms 113–118. Each of the six psalms expresses praise to the Lord. This collection of psalms was also called the *Egyptian* Hallel because it spoke of deliverance and salvation, especially deliverance from Egypt (see Psalm 114).

The context of the Great Hallel is deliverance from bondage in Egypt, which to the New Testament saint relates to deliverance from sin. Both are a form of redemption accomplished by God, with the Exodus foreshadowing the great redemption of humankind.

There are similarities between Psalm 118 and Moses' great song of deliverance recorded in Exodus 15. The Israelites not only saw but experienced the wall of water on each side as they walked on dry ground through the sea, followed by the drowning of all of Pharaoh's army. It was, indeed, a great deliverance, *the* great deliverance in the history of God's people and has always represented the great deliverance from sin of God's people through the cross and the empty tomb.

These similarities between Exodus 15 and Psalm 118 are striking:

The LORD is my strength and my defense;
　he has become my salvation.
He is my God, and I will praise him,
　my father's God, and I will exalt him.
　　　　　　　　　　Exodus 15:2

The LORD is my strength and my defense;
　he has become my salvation.
You are my God, and I will praise you;
　you are my God, and I will exalt you.
　　　　　　　　　　Psalm 118:14, 28

Also:

Your right hand, LORD,
  was majestic in power.
Your right hand, LORD,
  shattered the enemy.
                              Exodus 15:6

The LORD's right hand has done mighty things!
  The LORD's right hand is lifted high;
  the LORD's right hand has done mighty things!
                              Psalm 118:15b–16

Like the song of Moses, Psalm 118 praises God for his salvation. The psalm begins (v. 1) and ends (v. 29) with the same repeated, identical call to praise:

Give thanks to the LORD, for he is good;
  his love endures forever.

We are to praise God because he is good. The entirety of Psalm 118, what is sandwiched between the first and last verses, will reveal God's goodness.

All Who Know God's Lovingkindness
(Psalm 118:2–4)

Let Israel say:
"His love endures forever."
Let the house of Aaron say:
"His love endures forever."
Let those who fear the LORD say:
"His love endures forever."

The great example of his goodness is that his love (Hebrew *chesed*) endures forever. Repetition is powerful in Hebrew poetry, and in this case is intended to make a statement. The entire nation of Israel is invited to voice this praise (v. 2). This is something they all should be able to do. The priestly order of the nation is also invited to voice this praise (v. 3). They, of all people, should be aware and dedicated enough to voice this praise truthfully. Finally, all who fear the LORD are invited to voice this praise (v. 4). This refers to the entire nation again, but especially to those non-Jewish God fearers who have joined Israel in belief that the one true God is good. Indeed, the preceding psalm in the Great Hallel, Psalm 117, consists entirely of encouragement for all nations and all peoples to praise the Lord!

This progression through the nation, the priests, and the God-fearers has precedence in Psalm 115:9–11, another psalm of the Great Hallel, where the same three groups are invited to trust in the Lord, their help and shield. In Psalm 115:12–13 the same groups will be blessed by the Lord because he has "remembered us."

For a fuller example of thanking the Lord because his *chesed* love endures forever, all within the context of creation, a strong deliverance from Egypt, and the provision of the land through defeat of powerful kings, see Psalm 136.

It seems so innocent for all of us to praise God for his steadfast love, but as *Jesus* sang these words, especially on the night he was betrayed, he must have been very aware of the irony that God's faithful completion of his covenant with humankind required *him* to go to the cross.

The idea of a covenant being based on God's promise to fallen humankind began in Genesis 3:15

with Adam and Eve's first sin and God's promise that the offspring or seed of Eve, he (masculine, singular), would bruise or crush the head of the serpent. God's promise, even then, was backed by the shedding of blood of the animals God himself must have killed to clothe Adam and Eve (Genesis 3:21).

God's covenant love continued with his promises to Noah, promises that God clearly stated involved a *covenant* he initiated with Noah (Genesis 6:18). Part of God's instructions to Noah required him to bring two (a pair, or a male and his mate) of each kind of unclean animal into the ark, but to bring *seven pairs* of clean animals (Genesis 7:2). Why so many clean animals? How did Noah know which were clean and which were unclean? Based on God's preflood judgment that Noah was a righteous man and on Noah's thank offering of clean animals after the flood, there must have been knowledge of God's requirement for sacrifice of clean animals even before the flood. The number of clean animals on the ark ensured sufficient numbers for Noah to offer an acceptable sacrifice to God upon leaving the ark, as well as acceptable sacrifices for generations to come.

In response to Noah's sacrifice (Genesis 8:20ff), God promised to 1) never again curse the ground because of the evil ever present in men, 2) never again strike down every living creature, and 3) continue seedtime and harvest, summer and winter as long as the earth remained. He gave to humans everything for food, but established that he would require a reckoning for the life of a human being. In Genesis 9:9ff, God established his covenant with Noah, his descendants, and with every living creature that he would never again destroy the entire earth with a flood.

In pursuit of fulfilling his promises through the ages, God initiated a covenant with Abraham that he would bless Abraham, and that all nations or families of the earth would be blessed through Abraham (Genesis 12:3). After providing the substitutionary sacrifice for Isaac, God again promised to bless Abraham and told him that in his offspring all the nations of the earth would be blessed (Genesis 22:15–18). Psalm 118 reflects the fulfillment of that promise through the sacrifice of God's Son.

When the time in Egypt was fulfilled, Abraham's descendants were delivered and given the Promised Land. God promised Moses that he would deliver them from Egypt and he did it in a mighty way, with his "strong right arm." This is how God set the scene for the coming of his Son.

Eventually, God made the promise to David that he would establish the throne of David's son forever and not take his steadfast love from him as he took it from Saul. Here is the promise, based on God's eternal faithfulness and steadfast covenant love, that New Testament saints rely on. Here is the promise from God that he will never withdraw his love from Jesus and that the throne of Jesus will endure forever. Here is God's promise that all who believe in Jesus will have his eternal love under the eternal reign of Jesus. This is recorded, prophetically, by Ethan the Ezrahite in Psalm 89:

> [20] *I have found David my servant;*
> *with my sacred oil I have anointed him.*
> [21] *My hand will sustain him;*
> *surely my arm will strengthen him.*
> [22] *The enemy will not get the better of him;*
> *the wicked will not oppress him.*
> [23] *I will crush his foes before him*
> *and strike down his adversaries.*
> [24] *My faithful love will be with him,*
> *and through my name his horn will be exalted.*
> [25] *I will set his hand over the sea,*
> *his right hand over the rivers.*

²⁶ *He will call out to me, 'You are my Father,*
 my God, the Rock my Savior.'
²⁷ *And I will appoint him to be my firstborn,*
 the most exalted of the kings of the earth.
²⁸ *I will maintain my love to him forever,*
 and my covenant with him will never fail.
²⁹ *I will establish his line forever,*
 his throne as long as the heavens endure.

³⁰ *"If his sons forsake my law*
 and do not follow my statutes,
³¹ *if they violate my decrees*
 and fail to keep my commands,
³² *I will punish their sin with the rod,*
 their iniquity with flogging;
³³ *but I will not take my love from him,*
 nor will I ever betray my faithfulness.
³⁴ *I will not violate my covenant*
 or alter what my lips have uttered.
³⁵ *Once for all, I have sworn by my holiness—*
 and I will not lie to David—
³⁶ *that his line will continue forever*
 and his throne endure before me like the sun;
³⁷ *it will be established forever like the moon,*
 the faithful witness in the sky."

Through the prophets, God continued to announce that he was going to be faithful to his covenant love to Israel and to the world. So it is *God's* hand that has accomplished our salvation. Thus, the name of the Lord (*YHWH* or *YH*) is used more times in Psalm 118 than in any other.

In Isaiah 55:3 we are told of this everlasting covenant:

> *Give ear and come to me;*
>   *listen, that you may live.*
> *I will make an everlasting covenant with you,*
>   *my faithful love promised to David.*

Jesus and the Father were and are One, and Jesus certainly knew his Old Testament scriptures. As he sang these words of praise, on the night he was betrayed, he knew exactly what it would take to maintain God's faithful love forever, and to enable the true praises of his people for that faithful love to continue: it would require the sacrifice of his Son.

The LORD is with Me in My Distress
(Psalm 118: 5–7)

When hard pressed, I cried to the LORD;
he brought me into a spacious place.
The LORD is with me; I will not be afraid.
What can mere mortals do to me?
The LORD is with me; he is my helper.
I look in triumph on my enemies.

As with many of the psalms, the author of Psalm 118 often moves back and forth between first, second, and third person. In Psalm 118 the author switches to first person in verse 5. Many other psalms also relate the experience of crying out to God and being delivered. Who is this person in Psalm 118 whom the LORD has helped? We are not given the author's name but there are many clues within the psalm. We know that later in the psalm, he is leading the procession up to the temple to offer a sacrifice. He is most likely someone important such as a king, perhaps David himself. He rejoices in the victorious deliverance God has provided and invites others to join him in praise. Leading the people in a thanksgiving offering for deliverance from enemies is a clear reference to a person of royalty.

Being "hard pressed" or "in straits" is related to being in a tight spot. The author cries out to God from his position of not having room to move, to maneuver, to fight, and not having options. The contrast to God's answer is significant. God responds by giving him room, bringing him into a spacious place. Since the Lord is with him, he need not be afraid. After all, he is fighting mere mortals and he has God's help on his side. With God as his helper ("The Lord is with me" is stated in verse 6 and repeated in verse 7), he is able to look in triumph on his enemies. This language gives us the clue that the author was a warrior king like David.

It is interesting that the author of Hebrews chose Psalm 118:6 as a reminder to believers to lead a holy life. Perhaps to the persecuted church it is good to know that mere mortals can do little to actually harm followers of Christ. We fear only God and he, according to Hebrews 13:5, will never leave us or forsake us. Hebrews 13:6 is one of the significant

New Testament quotes from Psalm 118: "The Lord is my helper; I will not be afraid. What can mere mortals do to me?"

Surely this was of comfort to our Lord as he looked ahead to the ridicule, to the abuse, to the suffering and pain of death that the Father required of him: God was his helper and would be with him.

Put Your Trust in God, Not in Humans
(Psalm 118: 8–9)

It is better to take refuge in the Lord
than to trust in humans.
It is better to take refuge in the Lord
than to trust in princes.

The synthetic parallelism of verses 8 and 9 is notable. The first part of each verse is exactly the same, but the second part is stepped up in verse 9. Verse 9 goes one step further than verse 8. It is better to take refuge in the Lord than to trust in humans. Indeed, even trusting *princes* is not as good as trusting in the Lord. Certainly there was no one in whom Jesus could trust as he approached the cross. He knew that all would flee and deny him. From the beginning, he knew what was in people's hearts and did not entrust himself to them (John 2:24–25).

As Jesus sang this psalm on the night he was betrayed, he knew that even Peter, who claimed that he would go to the death with Jesus, would deny him three times. He knew that Judas was in the very act of betraying him and that all would flee, leaving him alone to face his enemies. His trust was in his Heavenly Father.

Surrounded by Enemies, the LORD Helped Me
(Psalm 118:10–12)

All the nations surrounded me,
but in the name of the LORD I cut them down.
They surrounded me on every side,
but in the name of the LORD I cut them down.
They swarmed around me like bees,
but they were consumed as quickly as burning thorns;
in the name of the LORD I cut them down.

Jesus knew he would be surrounded by his enemies. So thickly do they swarm around him in Psalm 118 that they are likened to bees. In Psalm 22, another clearly messianic psalm, the wicked surrounding him are referred to as bulls, strong bulls of Bashan (Psalm 22:12), as ravening and roaring lions (Psalm 22:13), as dogs (Psalm 22:16), and as wild oxen with horns (Psalm 22:21). In Psalm 118 the verb for "surround" is used three times (in the beginning of verses 10, 11, and 12).

Yes, Jesus knew what to expect in the Passion and crucifixion, but he also knew he would not cut them down as described in Psalm 118. Though the author of the psalm made a strong statement by repeating that he cut them down (vv. 10, 11, 12), when Jesus sang these words, he entrusted future judgment to the Father.

Isaiah 53:7 says, "He was oppressed and afflicted, yet he did not open his mouth; he was led like a lamb to the slaughter, and as a sheep before its shearers is silent, so he did not open his mouth." According to Matthew 27:12–14, "When he was accused by the chief priests and the elders, he gave no answer. Then Pilate asked him, 'Don't you hear the testimony they are bringing against you?' But Jesus made no reply, not even to a single charge—to the great amazement of the governor." Mark 15:3–5 and Luke 23:9–10 also attest to this.

When he was crucified, rather than retaliating or pronouncing judgment, Jesus said, "Father, forgive them, for they do not know what they are doing" (Luke 23:34). He blessed the repentant thief crucified beside him (Luke 23:43). He had come to announce the Good News and to offer salvation. He continued to the end to make intercession for sinners (Isaiah 53:12), as he does today.

The LORD's judgment and vengeance is reserved for a future time. Referring to himself, Jesus quoted psalms such as Psalm 110:1 "Sit at my right hand until I make your enemies a footstool for your feet" (Matthew 22:41–45, Mark 12:35–37, Luke 20:41–44). In the same psalm, Psalm 110:5–6, the day of the LORD's wrath is described: "…he [the LORD] will crush kings on the day of his wrath. He will judge the nations, heaping up the dead and crushing the rulers of the whole earth." For now, we live in a time of grace wherein there is still time for *anyone* to believe in the name of the Lord and be saved (Romans 10:13), but it will not always be so.

The LORD has Become my Salvation
(Psalm 118:13–14)

I was pushed back and about to fall,
but the LORD helped me.
The LORD is my strength and my defense;
he has become my salvation.

Psalm 118 is a psalm of praise, but a possible list of clues to also labeling it a *messianic* psalm might include references to the king, the throne, the anointed, the rule of God, defeat of enemies, or being quoted in the New Testament. So even though this psalm doesn't specifically mention a king or throne or the royal reign, it can be classified as a royal or messianic psalm because of the reference to defeating enemies, and also to the fact that it is quoted or referred to in the New Testament so many times.

When I read the words of verse 13, "I was pushed back and about to fall, but the LORD helped me," I think of the many ways in which Jesus knew his

Heavenly Father had strengthened him and prepared him for what lay ahead. From the temptation in the wilderness, full of the Holy Spirit and attended by angels (Matthew 4, Mark 1, Luke 4), to the great transfiguration in the presence of Moses and Elijah (Matthew 17, Mark 9, Luke 9), the Father was preparing his Son, *our Messiah.* In Luke 22:43, an angel appeared on the night of Christ's betrayal as he struggled in prayer in the garden. That angel was sent to strengthen him.

God would help Jesus on the cross, and would become his salvation. Even more significant, is the knowledge Jesus carried with him that, as the Father would be his salvation, he himself would become our salvation.

The Strong Right Hand of the LORD
(Psalm 118: 15–16)

Shouts of joy and victory
resound in the tents of the righteous:
"The LORD's right hand has done mighty things!
The LORD's right hand is lifted high;
the LORD's right hand has done mighty things!"

Ah! Victory! Shouts of joy and victory resound: the enemies are defeated! Here is the reference to the deliverance from Egypt: it is the LORD's right hand that has done it! The Hebrew phrase is used three times. When Israel left Egypt, left all their enemies behind, they did not have to fight for their freedom, for their salvation. God did it. There is not a more obvious or a more complete picture of the grace of God. Psalm 105 is quick to remind us that God's actions were a result of his commitment to the covenant he made with Abraham. God delivered them "laden with silver and gold" (Psalm 105:37), with the spoils of a war they didn't fight. God guided them and provided food and water for them. Battles would come later, but God brought them out with shouts of joy (Psalm 105:43).

Jesus knew he was expected to win our salvation for us, a most amazing act of God's grace, greater even than the Exodus. In keeping with his covenant promises, God would provide the substitutionary sacrifice for the world. Only God could accomplish so great a salvation! Only God's strong right hand could accomplish something so mighty. How shall we escape if we ignore (neglect) so great a salvation (Hebrews 1–2)?

I Will Not Die but Live
(Psalm 118:17–21)

I will not die but live,
and will proclaim what the LORD has done.
The LORD has chastened me severely,
but he has not given me over to death.
Open for me the gates of the righteous;
I will enter and give thanks to the LORD.
This is the gate of the LORD
through which the righteous may enter.
I will give you thanks, for you answered me;
you have become my salvation.

When my children were young, I was scheduled for a biopsy and cried out to God, asking that I be allowed to raise my children. Many people prayed for me and over me. God answered by giving me Psalm 118:17–18 as a clear answer to my prayers, thus beginning my enduring interest in Psalm 118. I would not die, but live to proclaim what the Lord had done.

When I went in for the biopsy, they could not find anything to biopsy! There were no lumps where there had been multiple lumps. Praise be to God! Today, at the age of 69, I am dying of cancer. Praise be to God, I have lived to see my grandchildren and to be spiritually influential in their lives.

As Jesus sang this song for the last time, he knew he *would* die unless the Father provided some other way. He struggled in prayer, asking that if possible this cup might be taken from him. Nevertheless, not his will, but the will of the Father superseded all. I still pray that this cup of suffering and death might pass from me, but I draw comfort from the fact that Jesus has gone before me in death. Not only in death, but in suffering, Christ has gone before me. Somehow, he will give me the inner strength to endure the kind of death he has ordained for me. God's will be done.

Jesus knew he was able to lay down his life of his own volition, but he also knew he could take up his life again, on authority granted by his Heavenly Father (John 10:17–18). So yes, he would die the physical death we will each experience, but he knew he would be resurrected and not die the second death (Revelation 21:7–8). He knew, as the firstfruits of

God (1 Corinthians 15:20), that he would go before us, providing resurrection and eternal life for those who believe in him. He could endure the cross for the joy set before him (Hebrews 12:2). So too, can we endure the first death for the joy set before us in Jesus Christ.

The voice behind Psalm 118 is the king leading the worshipers up to the temple. God has delivered him and he lives to proclaim what the LORD has done! Open the gates of the temple! He is going in to praise God and to give him thanks.

Suddenly, as the worshipers approach the temple, there is one gate through which the righteous may enter. *This* is the gate of the LORD through which the righteous may enter (Psalm 118:20). *Jesus* is the gate through which all must enter heaven! Verse 21 says "you answered me; you have become my salvation." Here is God's answer to Christ's suffering: Jesus would become the gate of righteousness and God would provide salvation through the resurrection! God would not only provide salvation for his Son, but for all who follow him.

The Rejected Stone Becomes the Cornerstone
(Psalm 118: 22–24)

The stone the builders rejected
has become the cornerstone;
*the L*ORD *has done this,*
and it is marvelous in our eyes.
*The L*ORD *has done it this very day;*
let us rejoice today and be glad.

Now we come to the core of the psalm, the full-blown prophetic statement quoted by Jesus about himself in Matthew 21:42, Mark 12:10–11, and Luke 20:17: "The stone the builders rejected has become the cornerstone; the LORD has done this, and it is marvelous in our eyes." God foreordained that a stone the builders of the temple rejected would become chief or head cornerstone (*rosh pinnah*) of God's own temple. A greater salvation than the Exodus has been accomplished, and it is the Father who has made all of this possible. God accomplished it.

In the book of Job, we see the suffering of the righteous Christ foretold. God revealed in Job 38:6–7 that at the time of creation he laid the earth's foundations, and he "laid its cornerstone—while the morning stars sang together and all the angels shouted for joy." God established Christ as a stone (*even*), *the earth's* cornerstone (*pinnah*) at creation. What a beautiful picture of God's *chesed* love, his covenant lovingkindness in action before the world began!

To hear the morning stars singing together and all the angels shouting for joy? How my heart yearns to hear those sounds! Perhaps in heaven there will be a way to celebrate the event with them all over again.

In Isaiah 28:16, God told his rebellious people, "See, I lay a stone in Zion, a tested stone, a precious cornerstone for a sure foundation; the one who relies on it will never be stricken with panic." More literally, "I lay for a foundation in Zion a stone (*even*), a stone tried (*bochan*), a precious (*yaqar*) cornerstone (*pinnah*)."

This is not just any stone. This is not an untried, undependable stone. This is a tried, tested stone approved for use in the building as a cornerstone.

This is a precious, rare, or costly cornerstone. It is

splendid (related to glory) and weighty. It is highly valued. It is as rare and precious as the Word of the Lord was in the days of Eli (I Samuel 3:1).

How appropriate for Jesus to sing verse 24 for the final time, "The Lord has done it this very day; let us rejoice today and be glad." God has overruled the people's rejection of his Son. God has made Jesus the chief cornerstone. The day of salvation has come and the world will rejoice in this day of salvation. Today, quite literally, this day when Jesus would be betrayed and lay down his life for us!

Many translations don't connect *this day* with the day of salvation: "This is the day which the Lord has made." The NIV translation, "The Lord has done it this very day," avoids the trap of a generic day created by God for us to rejoice in. It is *this day of salvation* that verse 24 speaks of, not just a day with pleasant weather for us to enjoy! Hallelujah! The true cornerstone has been placed.

LORD Save Us!
(Psalm 118: 25–26)

LORD, save us!
LORD, grant us success!
Blessed is he who comes in the name of the LORD.
From the house of the LORD we bless you.

"Hosanna" has and had become an expression of praise, but this strong entreaty literally means to beseech (*anna*) and the plea is for the LORD to save us now! (*Anna Hosa-nna*!) The time is now! Please! This is what the crowds were saying in Matthew chapter 21 and Mark chapter 11 while they spread their cloaks and branches in the way of our Lord. In front and after Jesus, people shouted, "Hosanna! Blessed is he who comes in the name of the Lord! Blessed is the coming kingdom of our father David! Hosanna in the highest heaven!" The crowd was quoting from Psalm 118:25–26. In their exuberance for their king, they evidently quoted a variety of prophetic sources. Luke 19:38 adds, "Blessed is the king who comes in the name of the Lord! Peace in heaven and glory in the highest!" Matthew 21:4–5 and John 12:15 include the reference to Zechariah 9:9: "Rejoice greatly, Daughter Zion! Shout, Daughter Jerusalem! See, your king comes to you, righteous and victorious, lowly and riding on a donkey, on a colt, the foal of a donkey."

This was high praise meant for the coming king, and Jesus accepted their praise even though he would not allow them to make him king. It was Jesus' triumphal entry into Jerusalem and the crowds knew not what they did! They welcomed the King of kings and Lord of lords into his city.

In Luke 19:41–44, Jesus grieved over the city of Jerusalem. Weeping, he stated that the city would be destroyed because "you did not recognize the time of God's coming to you." According to Matthew 23:37–39, Jesus grieved over the city, saying, "Look, your house is left to you desolate. For I tell you, you will not see me again until you say, 'Blessed is he who comes in the name of the Lord.'" The city and especially the temple, where he was rejected by the religious leaders, will be left desolate, left without his presence. Perhaps they will not recognize him until his second coming when they realize who he is. Or, will there come a time when all Israel realizes who Jesus is and repents? And all Israel will be saved (Romans 11:26).

Jesus, knowing that he would complete the transaction and fulfill the covenant requirements, faced rejection and abandonment by all. How his heart must have ached for his people as he sang these words the crowds had spoken so recently: LORD, save us!

Taking the Sacrifice to the Altar
(Psalm 118:27–28)

The LORD is God,
and he has made his light shine on us.
With boughs in hand, join in the festal procession
up to the horns of the altar.
You are my God, and I will praise you;
you are my God, and I will exalt you.

The kingly worshiper who leads the procession rejoices that God has made his light shine on him and his people. Jesus, the "true light that gives light to everyone" had come into the world but the world did not recognize him (John 1). Now, *he* must lead the way to the sacrifice. His is the kingly voice and he himself is the sacrifice.

Both translations of verse 27, "Bind the festal sacrifice with ropes" and "With boughs in hand, join in the festal procession" are valid and appropriate. The time of the sacrifice has come and Jesus knows they are on their way to the horns of the altar. There will be no escape for the sacrifice. There will be no substitute. He *is* the substitute.

He can only praise his Father: "You are my God, and I will praise you." Repeated in synonymous parallelism, "you are my God, and I will exalt you."

We join Christ in singing the last phrase of Psalm 118. "Give thanks to the Lord, for he is good; his love endures forever." The Lord has fulfilled the good promise he made to the people of Israel and Judah in Jeremiah 33:11–16. A righteous branch has sprouted from David's line and he is called "The Lord Our Righteous Savior."

Conclusion

Why do I love Psalm 118? I love it because it led Jesus from praise, through the Passion, to praise. But it doesn't stop there. It leads *us* from praise, through the faith that claims God as our helper to a reminder that we can put our trust in God. It reviews past (and future) deliverance with the strong reminder that God himself becomes our salvation when we trust in him. His strong right hand has been shown to deliver in mighty ways, so mighty that we may rejoice in rescue from death. It reminds us that Jesus has become the gate of salvation, regardless of his earthly rejection, a marvelous deed accomplished by God and worthy of celebrating! It tells us that Jesus, the light of the world was led to the cross. It tells us that if we claim him as our God, we have no choice but to praise him when all is said and done.

> ***Give thanks to the Lord, for he is good;***
> ***his love endures forever.***
> ***Psalm 118:29***

Bibliography

Alden, Robert L. *Psalms*. 3 vols. Volume 3 Songs of Discipleship. Chicago: Moody Press, 1976.

Kidner, Derek. *Psalms 73–150*. 2 vols. Tyndale Old Testament Commentaries 14b. Madison: Inter-Varsity Press, 1973.

Ross, Philip S. *Anthems for a Dying Lamb*. Fearn, Ross-shire, Scotland, UK: Christian Focus Publications Ltd., 2017.

For More Information

For more information including updates about upcoming books, visit:

gailethulson.com

About the Author

Gaile Thulson holds an undergraduate degree from Wheaton College with double majors in Elementary Education and Biblical Archaeology, as well as a master's degree in Old Testament from Denver Seminary and two Master of Education degrees from the University of Northern Colorado. She loves learning and has enjoyed teaching a variety of subjects to a variety of ages in a variety of settings. Reading fiction is one of her favorite pastimes and, as a writer, she loves expressing her faith in Christ through the fiction genre, as well as nonfiction and poetry. Grateful for their spiritual heritage, she and her husband Mark enjoy passing the Christian values of their parents down to their own children and grandchildren.

Cup of Water Publishing

Giving a thirsty person a cup of water brings refreshment and can be lifesaving. Christ declared that such an action by his disciples would not go unrewarded. In the same way, giving a cup of spiritual water brings refreshment and can also be lifesaving. It is the mission of Cup of Water Publishing to give spiritual refreshment to any who are "thirsty" by making available material that is wholesome, Biblical, theologically sound, and edifying. Ultimately, our goal is to point the way to Jesus, the source of true spiritual water.

CPSIA information can be obtained
at www.ICGtesting.com
Printed in the USA
BVHW031148160822
644710BV00012B/272/J